Robbie Does His Best

Cherryl Bradshaw

Series Editor
Neville Grant

LONGMAN
Publishing for the Caribbean

Pearson Education Limited
Edinburgh Gate, Harlow,
Essex CM20 2JE, England
and Associated Companies throughout the world

© Addison Wesley Longman Limited 1996
All rights reserved. No part of this publication may be reproduced, stored in a retrieval system, or transmitted in any form or by any means, electronic, mechanical, photocopying, recording, or otherwise, without the prior written permission of the publishers.

The right of Cherryl Bradshaw to be identified as author of this Work has been asserted by her in accordance with the Copyright, Designs and Patents Act 1988.

First published 1996
Fourth impression 2004

ISBN 0 582 28823 1

Set in 18pt Newhouse Infant

Printed in Malaysia, PA

The Publishers' policy is to use paper manufactured from sustainable forests.

Illustrated by Tessa Richardson-Jones

It was a bright, sunny morning. Robbie Rabbit rubbed his eyes and sat up in bed.

"Oh!" he cried. "My head hurts.
My eyes hurt.
I feel hot and cold all over.
I can't go to school today."

So he went back to sleep.

When Mother Rabbit did not see him come for breakfast, she went to get him.

She looked for him in the bathroom.
But he was not there.

Then she looked for him in the bedroom.
And there he was, fast asleep in bed.

Robbie opened his eyes and held his head.
"I'm too sick to go to school today," he said.

"Robbie!" she cried,
"what are you doing in bed?"

"Today is a schoolday.
It is late!"

Mother Rabbit looked at his eyes.
His eyes looked bright and clear.

She felt his head.
His head was cool.

"All right," she said.
"I will take you to the doctor.
You are very sick."

So Robbie got up and got ready.
Then they left home.

On their way, they saw some of Robbie's friends.
They were going to school.

"Where are you going, Robbie?" asked Hoppity.
"Today is a schoolday.
Miss Emily is going to give us a . . ."

"Oh! Oh! Oh!" groaned Robbie.
"Mummy, I'm going to be sick.
My legs are getting tired.
Let us go now."

"Okay," said Mother Rabbit with a smile.
"Goodbye, boys.
Robbie is very sick.
We are going to see the doctor."

So Robbie and his mother went on their way.
They walked quickly down the street.

Soon they came to Doctor Rabbit's house.
They opened the door and went in.

"Good morning Robbie," said Doctor Rabbit.
"How can I help you this morning? What is the matter?"

"Oh Doctor, I'm very sick," moaned Robbie.
"I cannot go to school today."

So Doctor Rabbit took Robbie and his mother to the examination room.
He put Robbie on the bed.

"Let me look at you," he said. "Open your mouth."

He looked in Robbie's mouth.

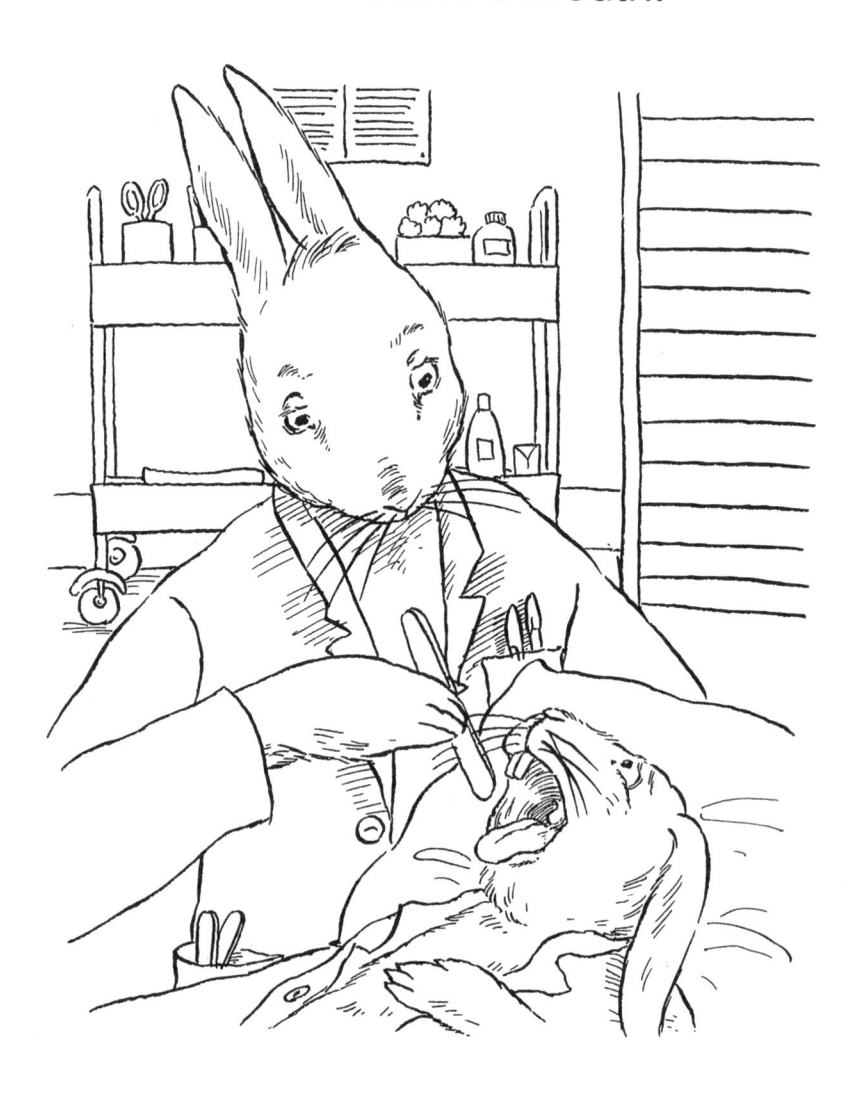

He looked in his eyes.
He felt his head.
He listened to his heart.

But everything was fine.

"Something is very strange here," he thought.
"Aha!" said Doctor Rabbit with a smile on his face.
"I know just what you need, and I have it right here."

Robbie saw Doctor Rabbit take out a needle.
Then he saw him take a bottle with something in it.

"No! No!" cried Robbie.
"I feel all better now.
I feel fine.
I'm not sick any more."

"Now, now, Robbie," said Doctor Rabbit.

"Do you want to tell me what is really wrong?

Why don't you want to go to school today?"

He sat down and looked at Robbie and waited.
Mother Rabbit also looked at Robbie and waited.

"Well . . ." said Robbie.
"Today is our day to spell words for Miss Emily.
I'm not good at spelling.
I get all mixed up."

"Did you learn the words for your spelling test?" asked Doctor Rabbit.

Robbie looked at his Mummy.
"Oh yes!" he said.
"Mummy helped me."

"Then all you have to do is your best," said Doctor Rabbit.

So Robbie climbed down from the bed, and walked over to Mother Rabbit.

"Mummy," he said, "I'm sorry. Is it too late to go to school now?"

Mother Rabbit looked at him and said, "No."

Questions

1. Why did Robbie say he did not want to go to school? What was the real reason? it wa.
2. Do you think his mother believed him? yes
3. What do you think happened after Robbie went to school?
4. Have you ever used the same excuse that Robbie used? When?
5. How would your eyes look when you are sick? When someone touches you, what would they feel?

Activities

Role-play some scenes from the story.

1. Robbie's mother asking him why he is still in bed and his actions when he answers.
2. Robbie's friends telling him what they will be doing at school and Robbie's reaction.
3. The doctor taking out the needle and Robbie's reaction.

Writing

Write another ending for the story saying how Robbie did the spelling test.